T0156745

GOD'S PLAN

Alpha & Omega of COVID 19

SALTY YEOM

Archway Publishing books may be ordered through booksellers or by contacting:

Archway Publishing
1663 Liberty Drive
Bloomington, IN 47403
www.archwaypublishing.com
844-669-3957

Scripture taken from the King James Version of the Bible.

ISBN: 978-1-4808-9596-6 (sc)
ISBN: 978-1-4808-9595-9 (hc)
ISBN: 978-1-4808-9597-3 (e)

Library of Congress Control Number: 2020917509

Print information available on the last page.

Archway Publishing rev. date: 10/13/2020

EPIGRAPH

Around early June 2020, I received a message from God about COVID-19. When I was in my thirties, I had been believing in God and Jesus diligently, and since then, I have been passionate about my work. Then, around the end of April 2020, my business stopped due to COVID-19. I prayed the creator to live, and 40 days after this, I received a message from God to write a book on COVID-19.

In short, the beginning and end of COVID-19 is the creator. COVID-19 is a creator and God's plan. So, to know the alpha and omega of COVID-19, you need to know the history of the creator. but,

It doesn't matter if you look from the middle of the book that you want to read.

GOD'S PLAN #1

«BASIC»
PLAN A

1

The Trinity

Before the earth, the universe, and the human beings were created, there was the nonmaterial world, the world of the spirit, different from the present world, the material world.

In the spirit world, God the Father, the Holy Spirit, and the Son existed first. They are called the Trinity.

2

The Plan of Creation

The Trinity planned to create a new spirit, different from the existing angels, that is, a spirit that most resembled the Trinity through a material world.

3

Plan Implementation

Creator Trinity first made a singular point, a hole leading from the nonmaterial system to the material system. And a big bang from this point created a material system from the nonmaterial system. After the big bang, the solar system and the earth were made, creating a place called Eden on earth.

4

The First Central Adam's Flesh and Adam's Spirit

The first central person to execute the Creator's plan was born in Eden and blessed to

- Be fruitful
- Multiply
- Replenish
- Subdue it

5

Archangels against the Creator's Plan

Archangel Luciel opposed the creation of a new spirit through the material world. In response, the Creator sent Luciel to Eden on earth, a material world, and gave him the mission of protecting Adam and Eve.

6

First Law and Adam's Disobedience

The Creator gave Adam the first law to fulfill the plan of creation. However, because of the interferer, Luciel—represented by a snake in the Bible—Adam broke the original law. The disobedience of the first centroid became the singularity of sin and resulted in a great explosion of sin.

7

The Seed of Sin and the Spread of Sin

The Creator inflicted various pains on Adam, and because of Adam's sin, the Creator drove him and his mate, Eve, out of Eden. They had their first son, Cain, outside Eden, and Cain committed the first murder. The Creator's first trial of the plan thus failed.

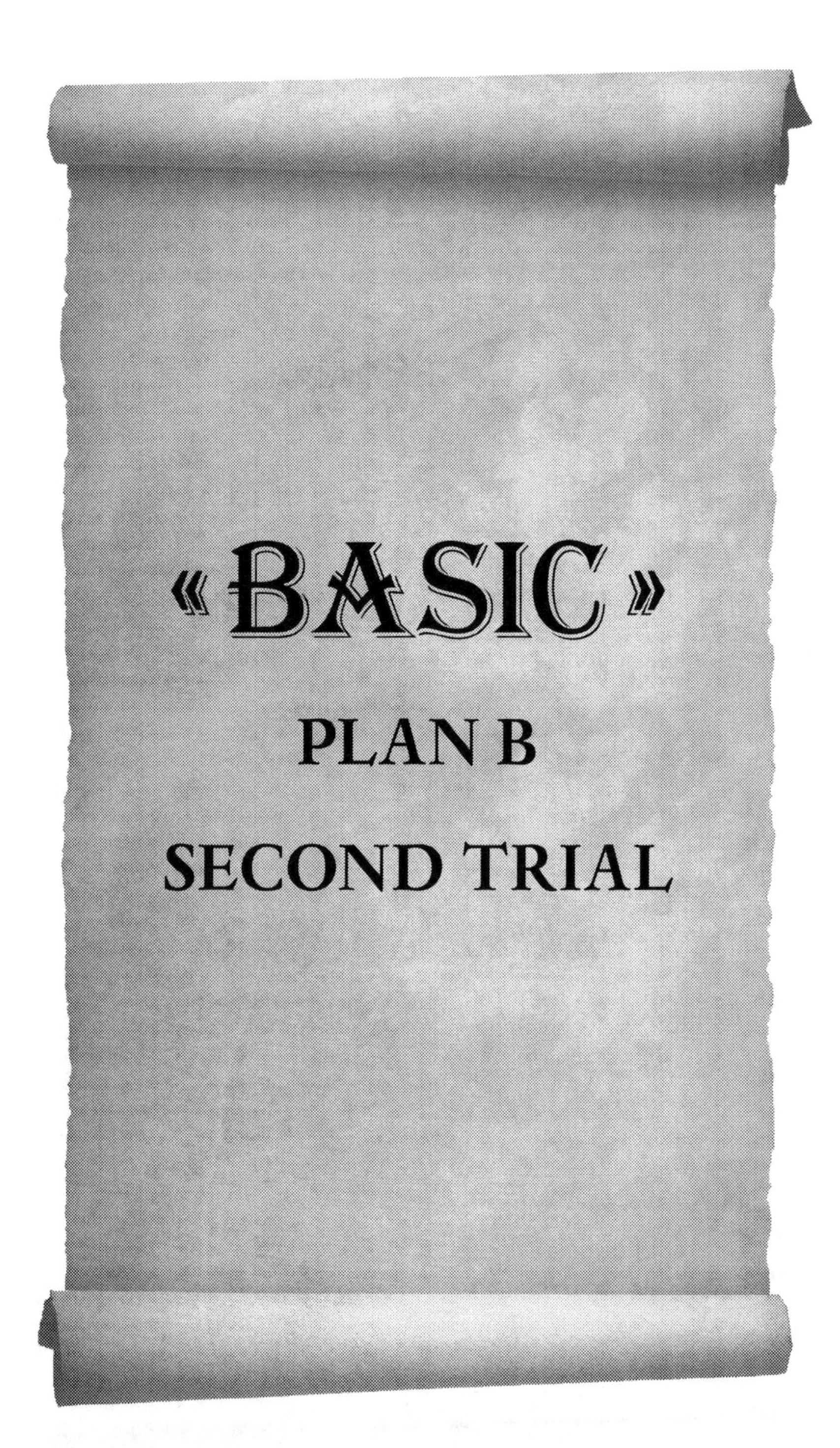
«BASIC»
PLAN B
SECOND TRIAL

1

Prepare the Second Adam and God's Plan

The sin of the first Adam caused a big bang of sin in humankind. To solve this and to fulfill God's plan, the Creator prepared the second Adam and established a period of preparation to meet him.

This was Plan B.

2

Second Adam: Jesus of Nazareth

Original sin was inherited. And until the second Adam, created to solve the original sin, all humankind was guilty of solidarity. The Creator sent the second Adam to earth to solve this problem of sin and to fulfill God's plan.

3

Obedience of the Second Adam and the Sin of Killing the Second Adam

The second Adam obeyed God's plan. However, the descendants of the original sin killed the second Adam, keeping him from completing God's plan.

4

The Second Trial of God's Ends, and the Third Trial Begins

Plan B ended because the second Adam in the middle of creation Plan B was killed by Satan and Satan's children. The Creator Trinity prepared Plan C, the third trial to achieving God's original plan.

«BASIC»

PLAN C

1

The Final Central Figure: the Third Adam

The Creator finally sent the third Adam, as he had Jesus, to earth to complete God's original plan of creating the new spirit that most resembled the Creator Trinity.

2

The Achievement of Plan C

As mentioned before, the second Adam's flesh was killed by Satan. So to achieve the God's plan, the last—the third—Adam was sent to earth. The final Adam was only united with the Trinity, opening the door to completing the original God's plan.

3

The Third Adam Opened the Door to Completing God's Plan

The third Adam opened the door to completing the Trinity plan while humankind was asleep because of the problem of sin. But again, humankind sinned without knowing the last man. The Creator Trinity sent a sign of the final battle to drive away human sin.

4

The Next Plan: Judgment and Disaster

The sins of Satan's descendants who imprisoned the third Adam included the sin of not accepting the word of the third Adam and original sin.

The Trinity must judge sin. The biggest sin is not to receive God's plan. But whoever receives God's plan and the third Adam will win against the disaster.

The following are the signs of judgment.

1. Wars, earthquakes, and poverty occur.
2. The Holy Spirit's work is evident.
3. The kings of the world fall.
4. Plagues hit: COVID-19 and more.

«DEEPER»

THEME 1

About the End of the World

For nation shall rise against nation, and kingdom against kingdom: and there shall be famines, and pestilence, and earthquakes. <Source: www.holybible.or.kr>

Matthew 24:7 KJV

1. War, famines
2. Pestilences, plagues
3. Earthquakes

Especially at the end of AD 2019, COVID-19 prevailed.

THEME #1:<POINT>

1. Except in the KJV Bible, there is no mention of the plague <*As a result of personally researching the Bible*>
2. Is COVID-19 God's judgment? Perhaps the plague?
3. Will there be more COVID? Perhaps COVID-20 or COVID-21 or COVID-22? Or might COVID-19 last longer?

The answers to these are later.

THEME #2

About Noah

1. God's sorrow to see sins of men.
2. God's decision to judge the sin.
3. Noah is a just man.
4. God said to only Noah, "Make an ark with God."
5. Into ark with family and animals before judgment.
6. God's judgment of humankind by flood.
7. Out of ark.
8. Restart with Noah.

Like Noah's age, like at Jesus's age, conditions are now repeating. Why?

THEME #3

What Is Adam?

Nevertheless death reigned from Adam to Moses, even over them that had not sinned after The similitude of Adam's transgression, who is the figure of him that was to come.

For as by one man's disobedience many were made sinners, so by the obedience of one shall many be righteous.

Romans 5:14–19 KJV

1. Adam is a core of God's plan.
2. Adam is different from Old Testament prophets, Adam is different from Jesus's apostles.

THEME #4

Who Am I?

When young, I listened to my father's word and studied hard to win the survival but not to the top (was difficult). After rest, I tried to win the other survival because I must get the job and wanted to help my family and to run away. But first trial failed.

Nearly died because of disease in lung at twenty-nine years old. After recovery a bit, I tried to win survival again. On the way, I met Jesus in the Bible (AD 2008). Jesus said to me, "I am the truth, the way, and follow me." Just I followed Jesus first of all.

Ten months later, I met another man who loves Jesus so much.

He was the third Adam.

When thirty-four to thirty-eight years old, I was with third Adam's group.

But suffering of economic problems etc. continued,

And I left him and his group at thirty-nine years old.

Go to abroad to live, but no way. I returned to hometown where my parent and family lived.

I taught math to earn money for six years, until April 2020.

From 2015 to 2020, I never prayed to God.

April 20 2020, I nearly died because of COVID-19, so I prayed to God,

"Love me, save me, or I will die."

At that time, I realized the reason for my suffering is first Adam's sin.

My prayer to God continued.

May 31, 2020

When tried to save wounded cat on the road,

The Holy Spirit came to me, and Third Adam's spirit came into me.

The Holy Spirit said to me,

"Make the book of God's plan and proof of the third Adam,"

And taught to me signs of a big disaster and judgement of sin and what is sin.

The Holy Spirit taught me about third Adam. From 2008 to 2018, the Third Adam was imprisoned for the salvation mankind.

Because of his sacrifice, I happened to meet Jesus at 2008,

And I came to know God's plan.

THEME #5

Temple Mount, Mount Moriah

<history>

If the diagram is not visible, you can pull or slide the screen cursor.

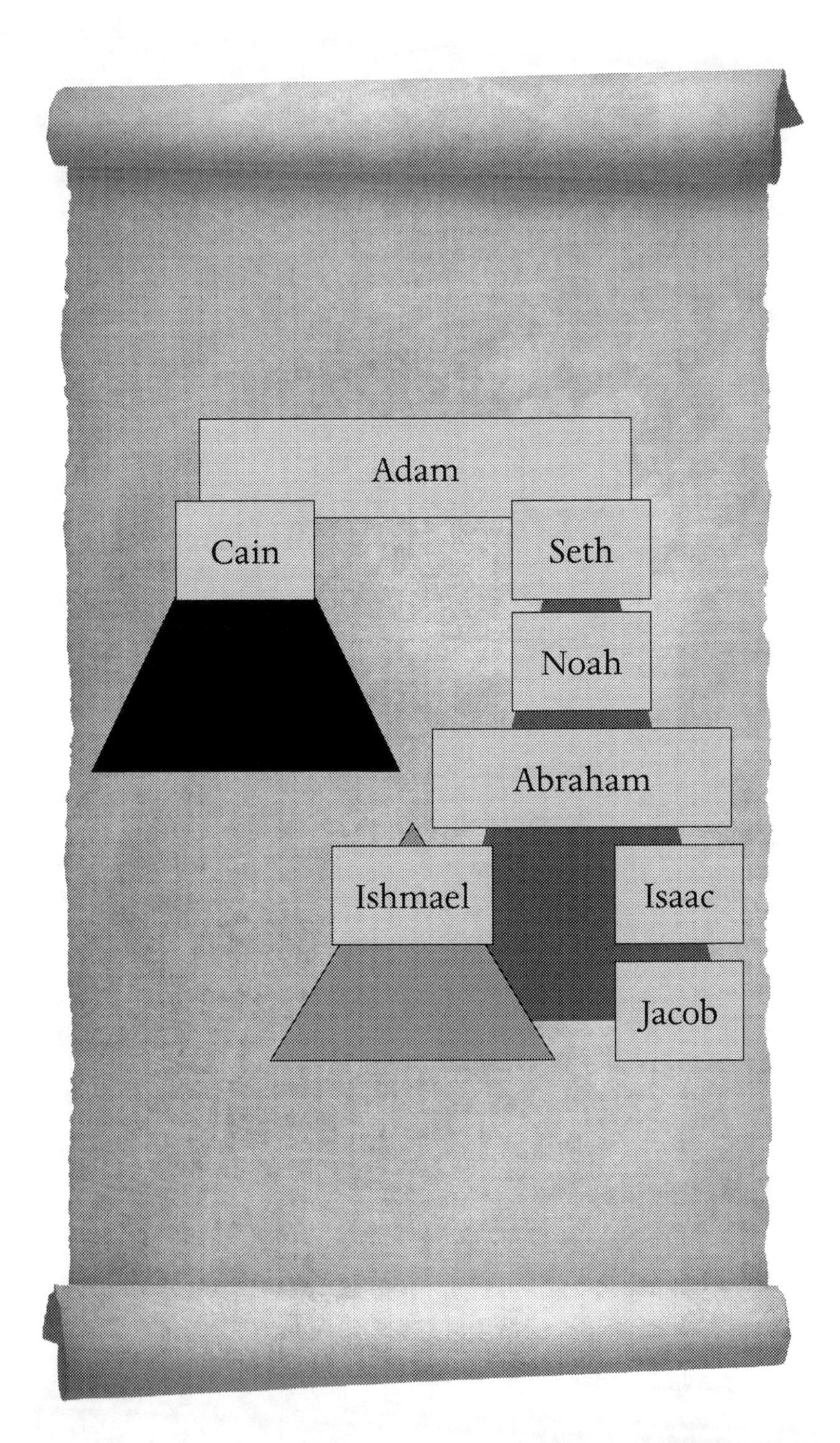
Adam
Cain
Seth
Noah
Abraham
Ishmael
Isaac
Jacob

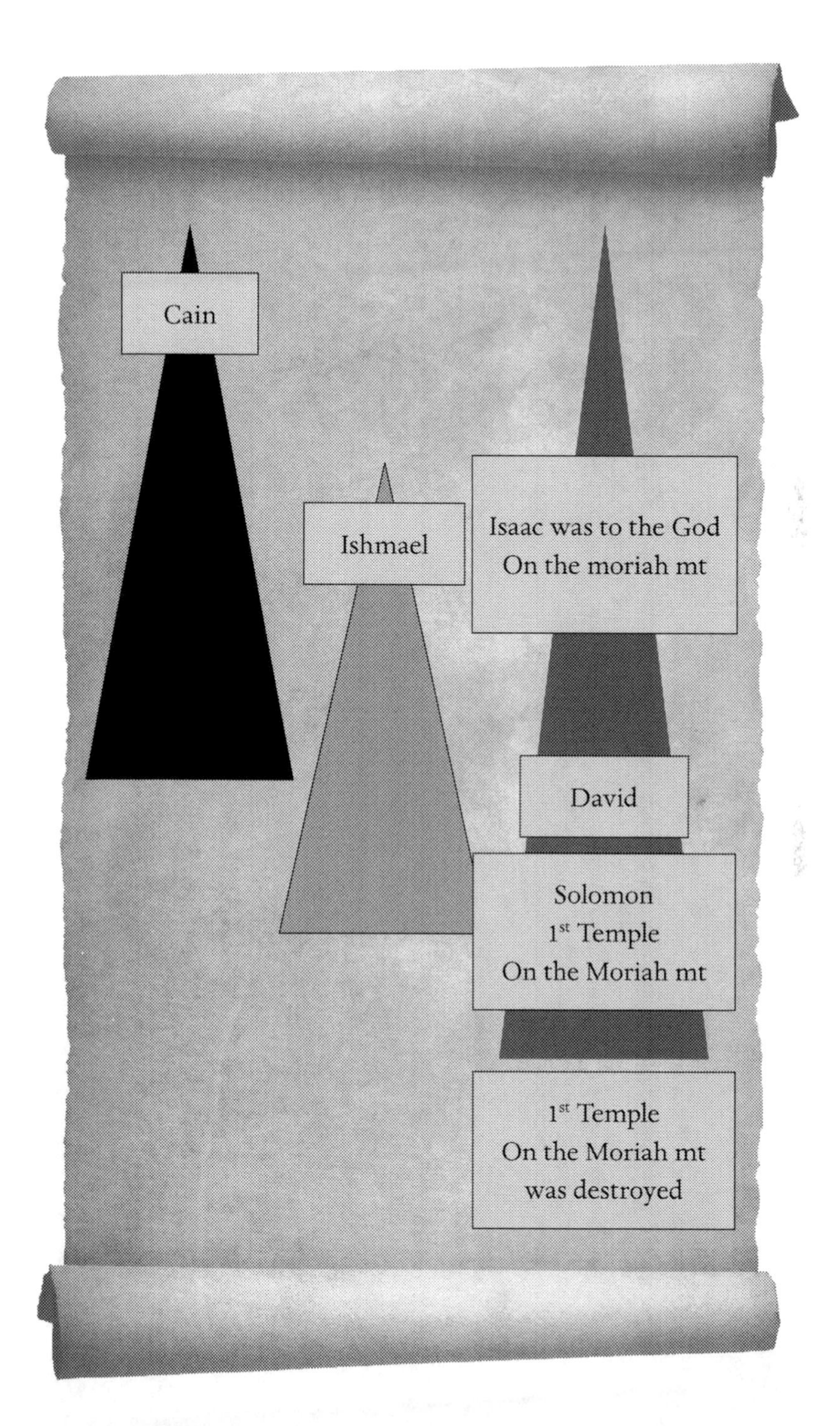
Cain
Ishmael
Isaac was to the God
On the moriah mt
David
Solomon
1st Temple
On the Moriah mt
1st Temple
On the Moriah mt
was destroyed

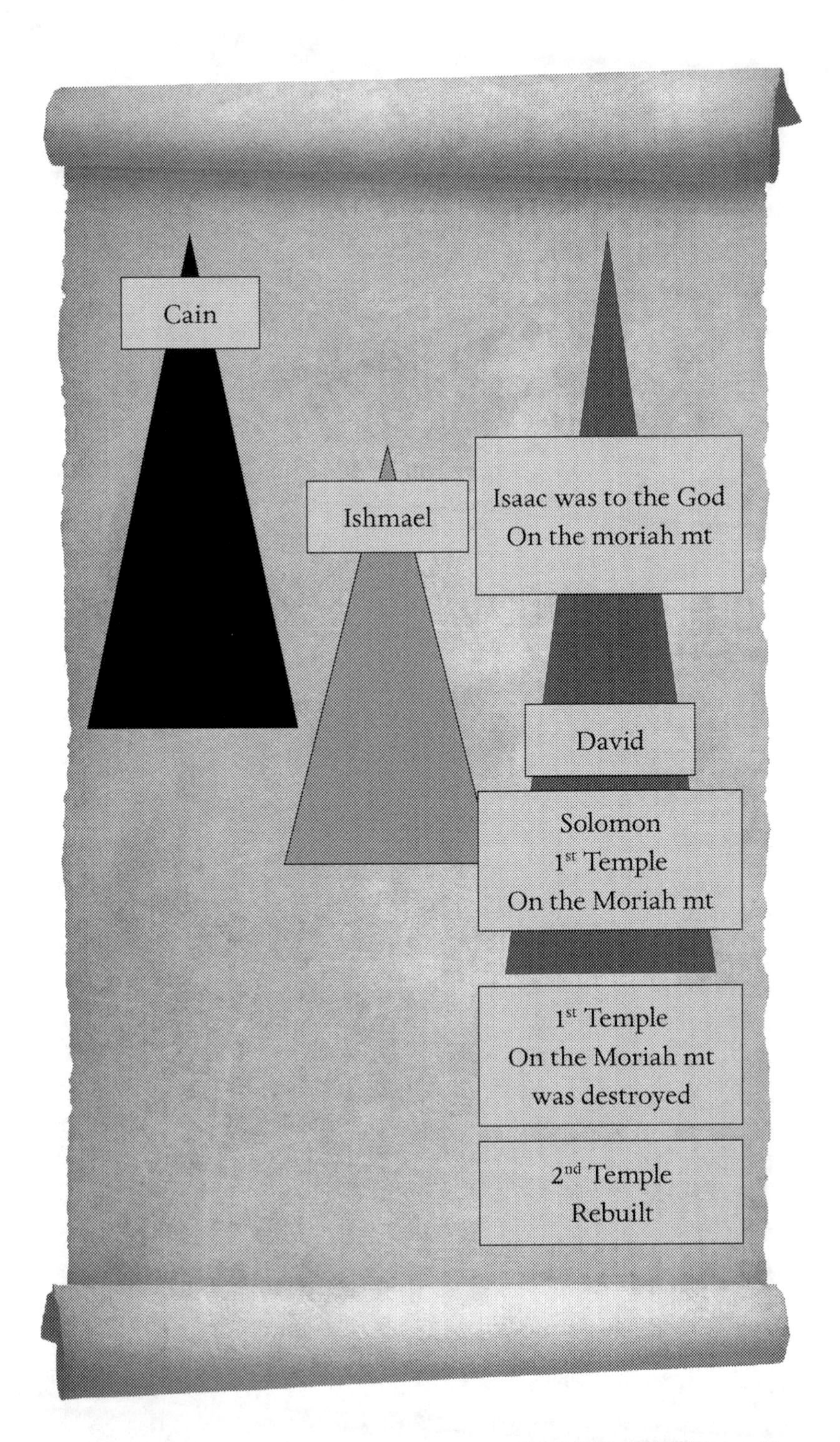
Cain
Ishmael
Isaac was to the God
On the moriah mt
David
Solomon
1st Temple
On the Moriah mt
1st Temple
On the Moriah mt
was destroyed
2nd Temple
Rebuilt

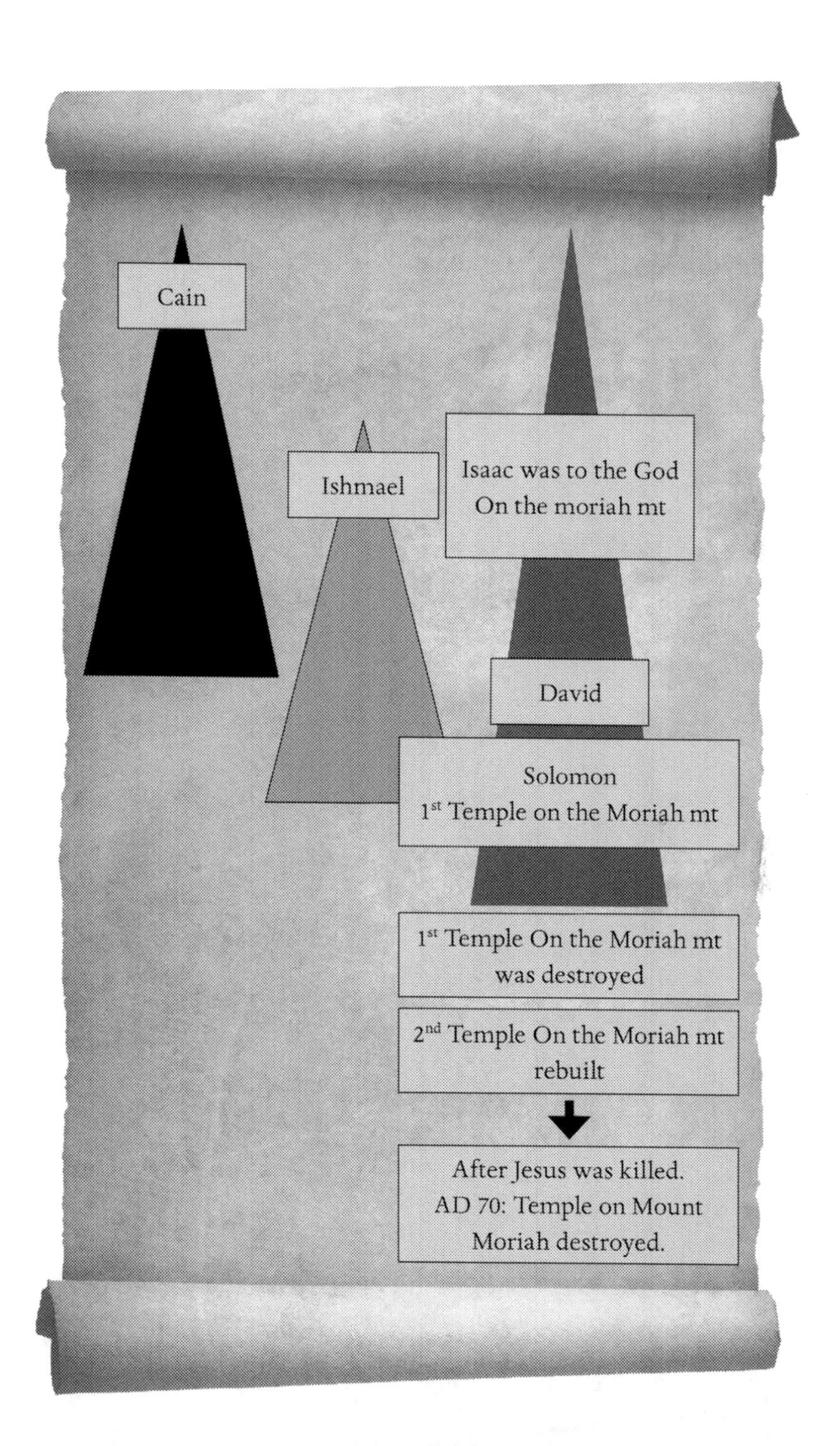
Cain
Ishmael
Isaac was to the God
On the moriah mt
David
Solomon
1st Temple on the Moriah mt
1st Temple On the Moriah mt
was destroyed
2nd Temple On the Moriah mt
rebuilt
After Jesus was killed.
AD 70: Temple on Mount
Moriah destroyed.

Cain
Ishmael
Isaac was to the God
On the moriah mt
David
Solomon
1st Temple on the Moriah mt
1st Temple On the Moriah mt
was destroyed
2nd Temple On the Moriah mt
rebuilt
After Jesus was killed.
AD 70: Temple on Mount
Moriah destroyed.
AD 688, the
Dome of the Rock
On Mount Moriah

MOUNT MORIAH

2000 BC (Abraham)–AD 688: With God's Servant

---->

AD 688–AD2020: Not with God's Servant

What happened?

The relationship with God was broken.

Why?

Instead of believing God's Word,
Abraham accepted his wife's word.
Like that, instead of obeying God's Word,
first Adam accepted his Hawa.
Seeds of sin caused big problem.
God must judge sin, especially of central man.
<Genesis 3:11-12 >

THEME #6

About the End of the World

When ye therefore shall see
the abomination of desolation,
spoken of by Daniel the prophet,
stand in the holy place.
Matthew 24:15 KJV

Then let them which be in Judaea
Flee into the mountains:
Matthew 24:16

But thou, O Daniel, shut up the words, and seal the book, [even] to the time of the end:
(Daniel 12:4)

And from the time [that] the daily [sacrifice] shall be taken away, and the abomination that maketh desolate set up,[there shall be] a thousand two hundred and ninety days.

Blessed [is] he that waiteth, and cometh to the thounsand three hundred and five and thirty days.
Daniel 12:11–12

1> AD 688

The Dome of Rock—the abomination of desolation—was the first Muslim masterpiece. It was built in about AD 688.

2> AD 688 + 1290 = 1978

3> AD 688 + 1335 = 2023

Through this fact, what did the Trinity want to say? < And from the time [that] the daily [sacrifice] shall be taken away, and the abomination that maketh desolate set up,[there shall be] a *thousand two hundred and ninety* days.

Blessed [is] he that waiteth, and cometh to the *thounsand three hundred and five and thirty* days.

Daniel 12:11–12>

All these things spake Jesus unto the multitude in parables; and without a parable spake he not unto them: that it might be fullfilled which was spoken by the prophet, saying, I will open my mouth in parables; I will utter things which been kept secret from the foundation of the world. (Daniel 13:34–35)

1. Parable: secret
2. The key to parable: third Adam à Day = Year
3. Like Noah's time, God said to center with God about judgment and the way to avoid the judgment.
4. God's algorithm to fulfill the plan is the same whenever.
5. So it seems that history is repeated.
6. God gives a law to humankind.

7. If receive, receiver grows more with God.
8. If not received, receives judgment; if repent, forgive and restart.

Because God created humans and all things.

QUESTIONS

1. AD 1978–AD 2023 means what?
2. Who is the central in this age?
3. What is the proof of the central, the third Adam?

ANSWERS

1. AD 1978.06.01–2023.06.01
2. The third Adam, with Trinity, is saving humankind and judging humankind's sin. Especially 2020.0601–2023.0601—COVID-19
3. The Trinity will decrease the judgment, especially to third Adam and those with him.

The proof of the central—the third Adam—will be that these predictions will come true.

THEME #7:

What to Do?

While I was praying, I received the next message from the Trinity.

The Trinity said,

"My israel and 2nd israel,
listen to my word
Go to your moutain not Moriah
And make your altar
Receive me
I am 1st Adam's God, Seth'God
Abraham's God, Issac's God
Jacob's God,David's God, Solomon's God,
Nasaret Jesus's God
And your eternal God."

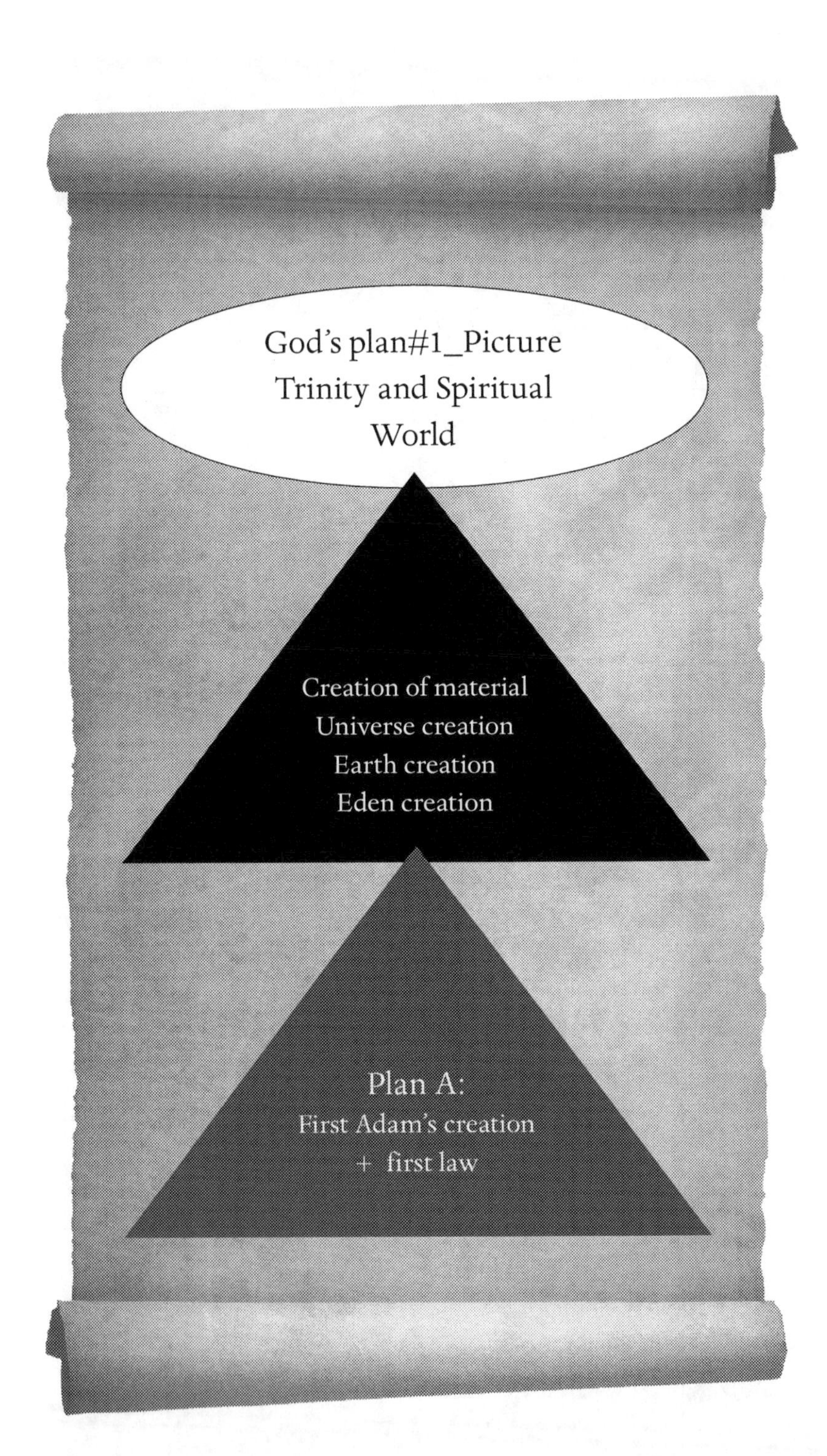
God's plan#1_Picture
Trinity and Spiritual
World
Creation of material
Universe creation
Earth creation
Eden creation
Plan A:
First Adam's creation
+ first law

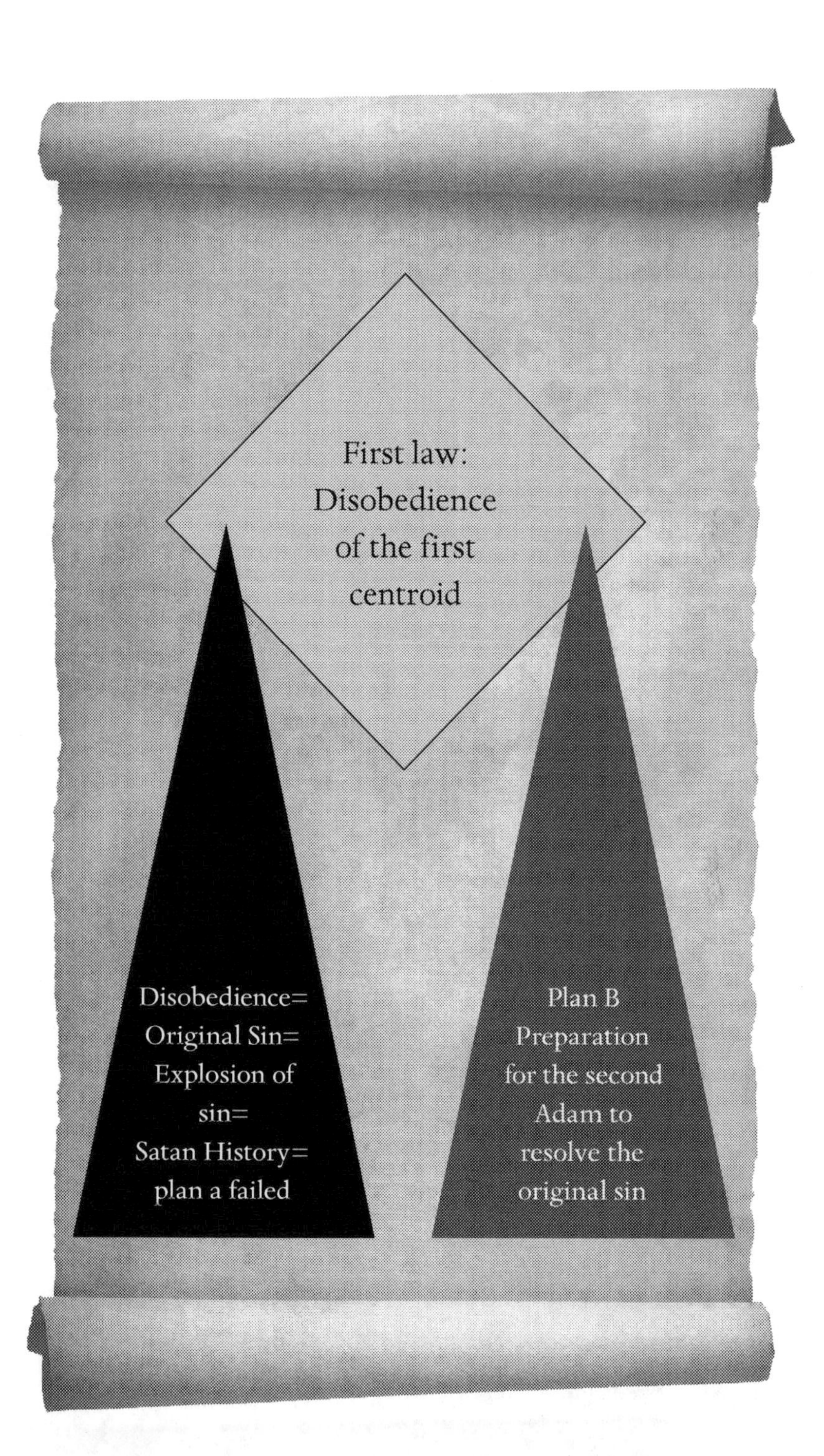
First law:
Disobedience
of the first
centroid
Disobedience=
Original Sin=
Explosion of
sin=
Satan History=
plan a failed
Plan B
Preparation
for the second
Adam to
resolve the
original sin

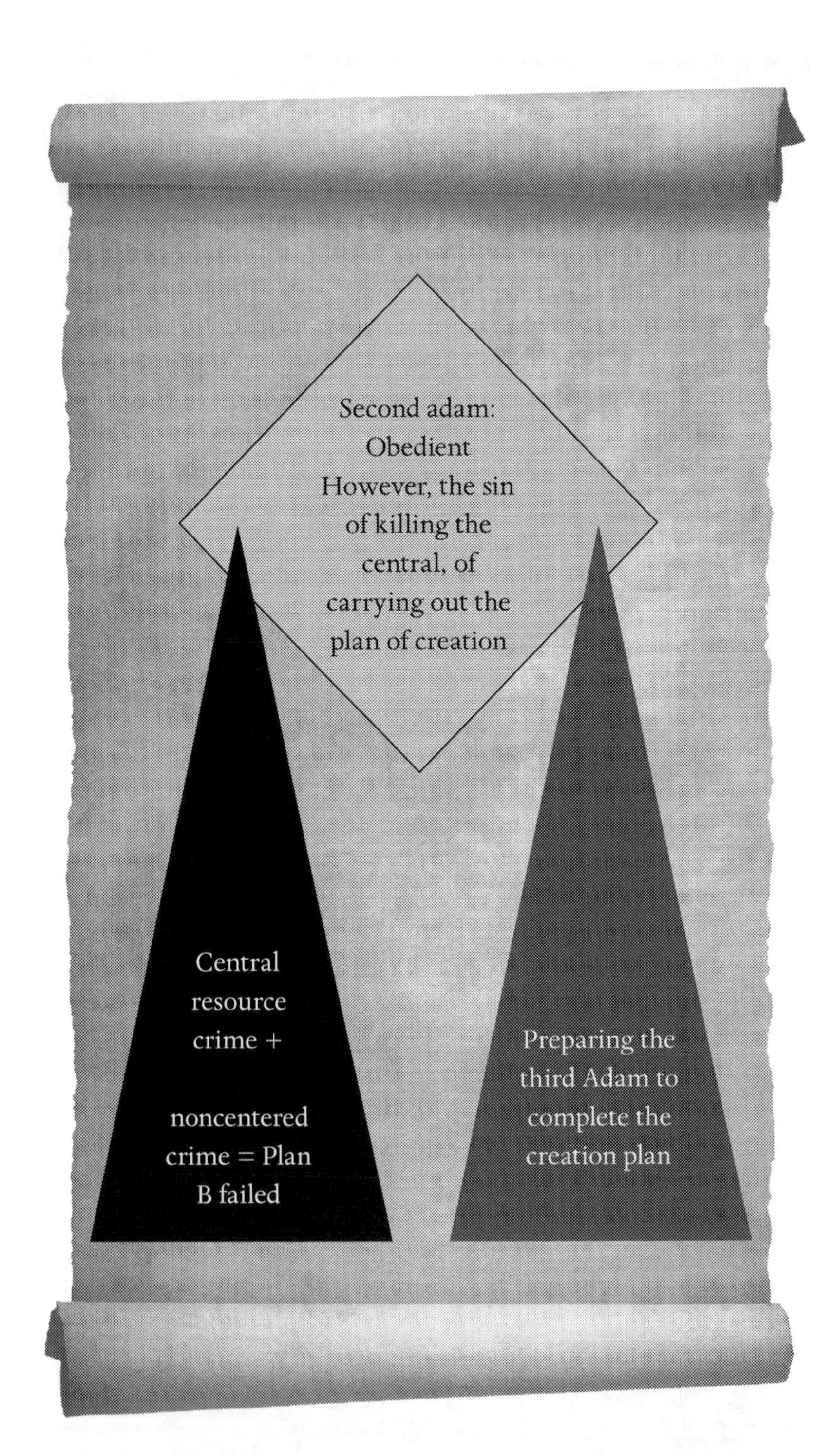
Second adam:
Obedient
However, the sin
of killing the
central, of
carrying out the
plan of creation
Central
resource
crime +
noncentered
crime = Plan
B failed
Preparing the
third Adam to
complete the
creation plan

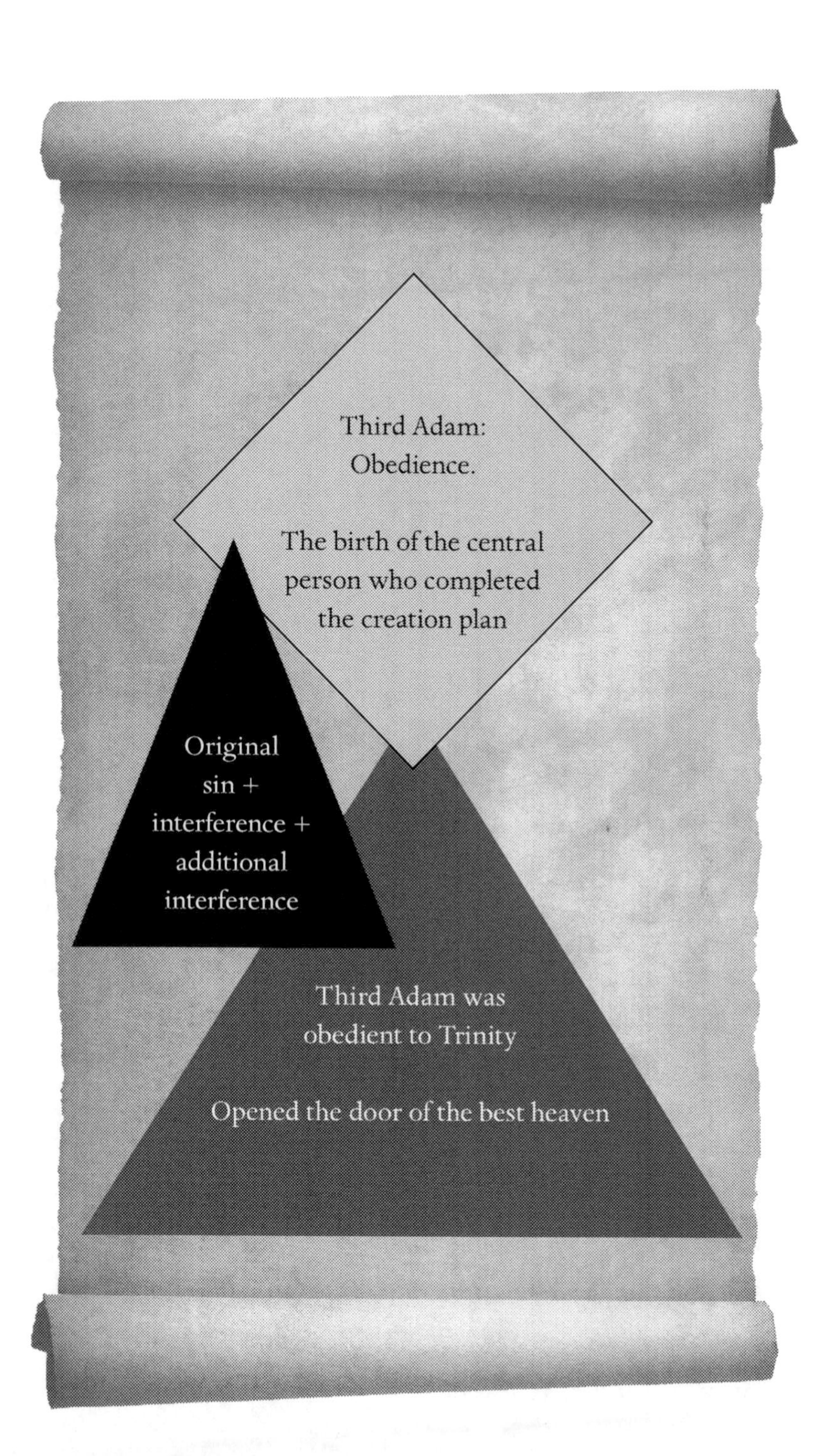
Third Adam:
Obedience.
The birth of the central
person who completed
the creation plan
Original
sin +
interference +
additional
interference
Third Adam was
obedient to Trinity
Opened the door of the best heaven

Final Mission for Creation Planning:

Judgment to destroy Satan, his children, and all they have done illegally.

Signs: wars, earthquakes, poverty, plague = COVID-19 (2020–2023), the work of the Holy Spirit, the fall of world kings.

GOD'S PLAN #2

COVID-19 VACCINES

1

Extreme suffering because of COVID-19 (coronavirus)

2

To avoid suffering, receive the vaccines.

3

COVID-19 is God's judgment.

4

Why judgment?

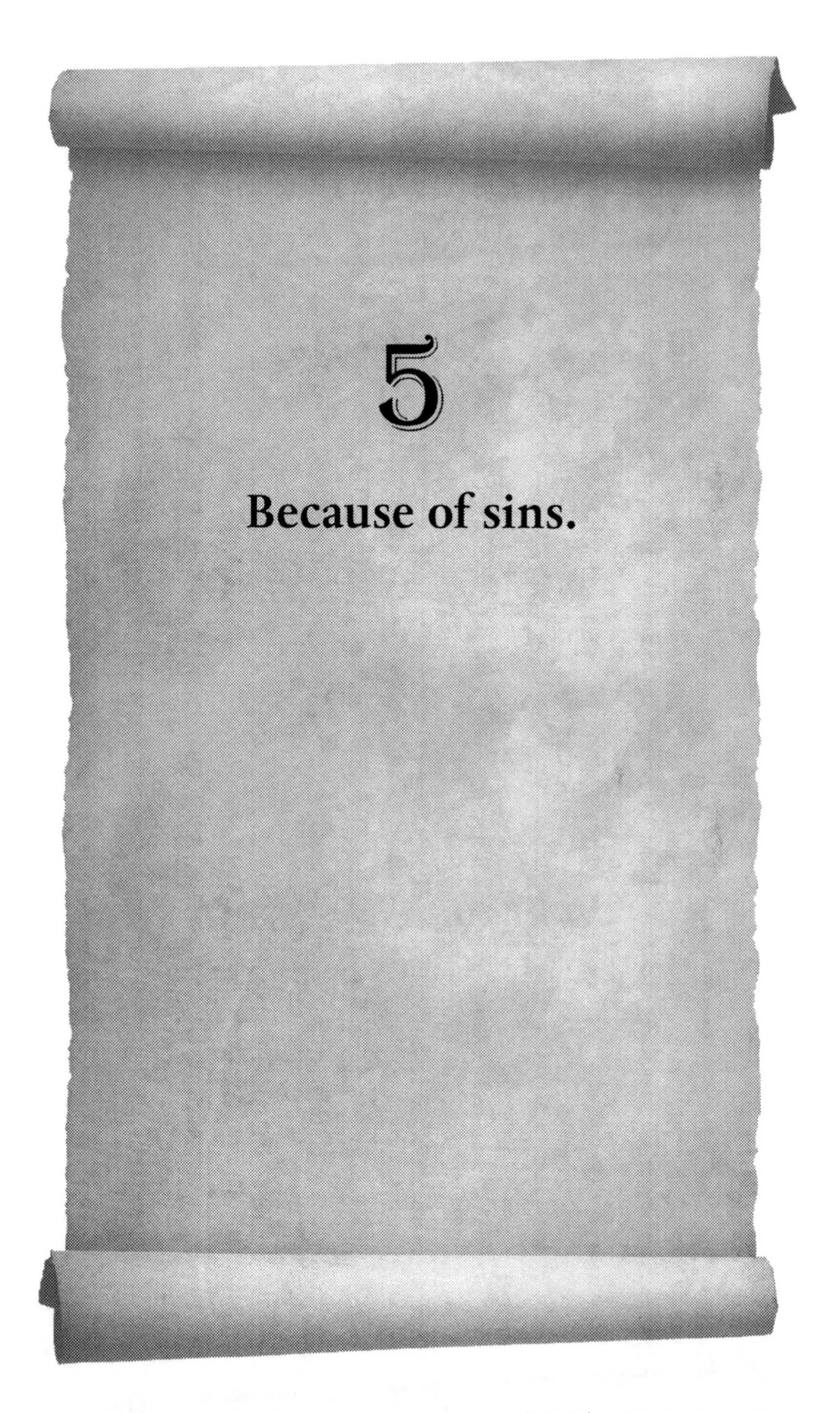
5
Because of sins.

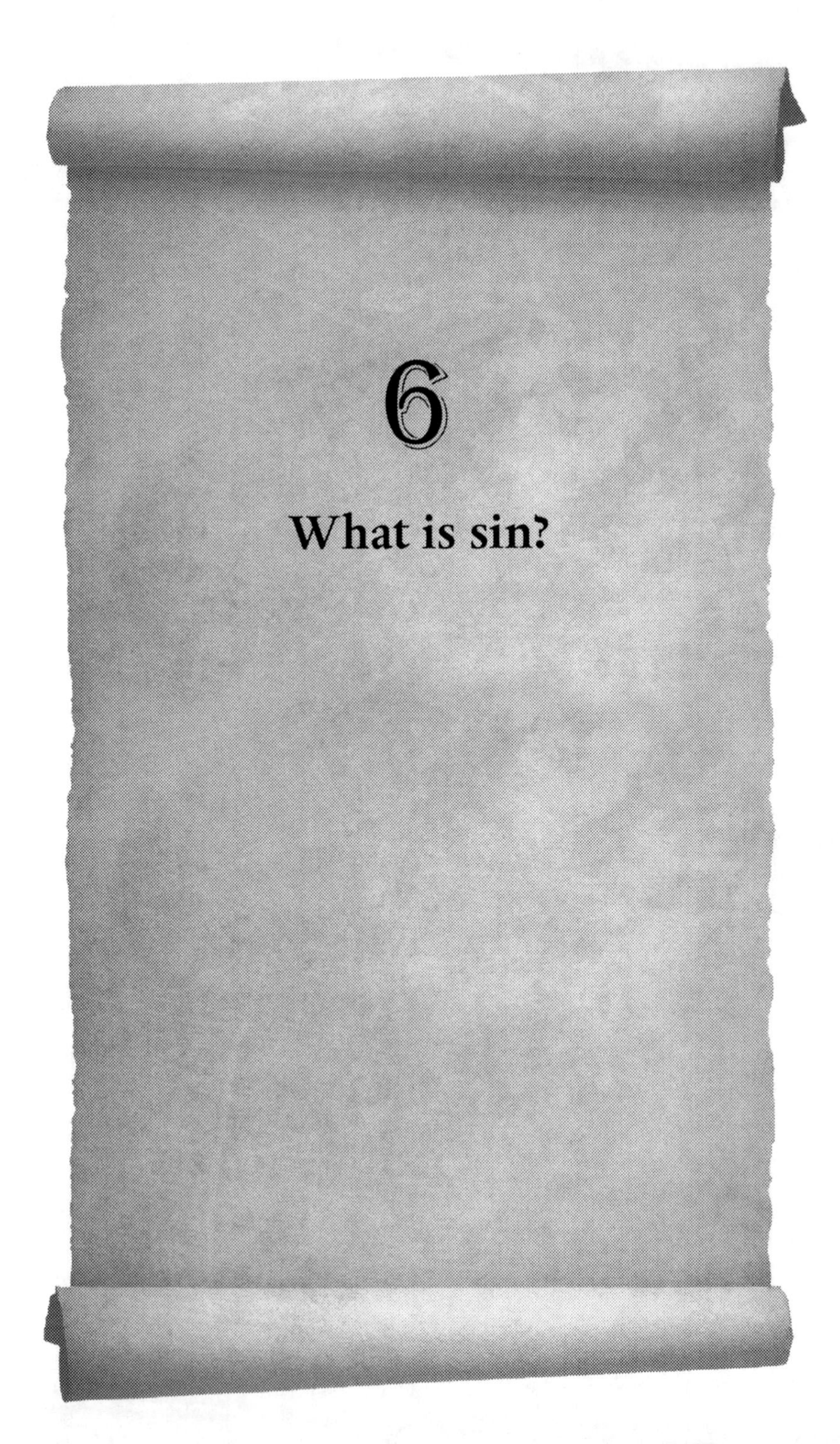

6

What is sin?

7

Sin is not knowing God's plan.

8

God's plan is the vaccine against COVID-19.

VACCINE
#1

<A message from the Trinity when I prayed for COVID-19.>

God's message about COVID-19:

My Israel and 2nd Israel, listen to my word
Go to your moutain not Moriah
And make your altar,
Receive me
I am 1st Adam's God, Seth'God Abraham's God,
Issac's God
Jacob's God,David's God, Solomon's God,
Nasaret Jesus's God
And your eternal God.

1

What is your Mt.?

—Your Mt. = not Moriah.

—Your Mt. = near.

—Your Mt. = God's plan.

Example: My Mt. = my birth town, left thirty-five years ago.

2

What is the altar?

—Altar = Where my old self died.

—Altar = Where my old knowledge died.

—Altar = Where my old lover died.

3

To receive God's plan:

If make your altar what God wants, you will receive God's plan, and the suffering of COVID-19 will decrease.

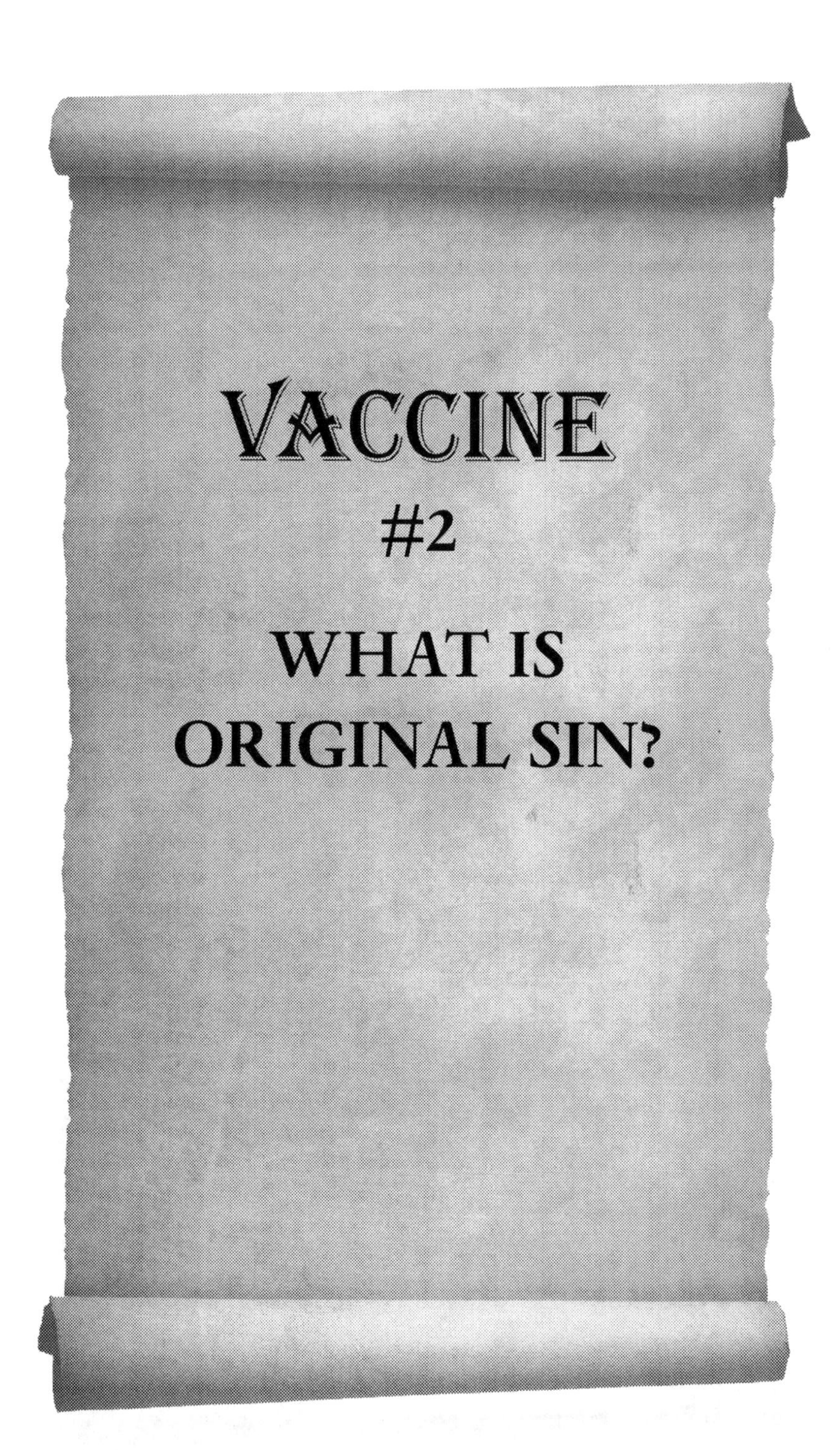

VACCINE
#2
WHAT IS ORIGINAL SIN?

1

About Original Sin

1. God created a central man as the first new spirit (spirit control body of flesh and soul, give a spirit order. So spirit is rotten → soul + flesh: rotten, or 2> usually soul rotten → flesh rotten = bad act → spirit rotten).
2. First man = Adam (not first of humankind) Adam's flesh (DNA, etc.) had been ready for long time
3. for making the new spirit.

4. Adam was born from his flesh parents, and when Adam's embryo is several weeks old, Adam's spirit (from spirit world or Holy Spirit) came into his flesh.
5. Adam has a flesh + soul (heart + thought) + spirit.
6. Spirit grows because of flesh + soul's work.
7. Spirit can be rotten.
8. God gave a law to make a seven-level spirit.
9. Maybe a law is a love promise between God and Adam.
10. If he obeyed a law (promise), Adam's spirit grew to the seventh level for his life limit and flesh: seven-level DNA + soul: seven-level DNA à multiply (flesh, spirit) → replenish.

11. If he did not obey a law, Adam's spirit would be rotten.
12. The result: Adam did not obey. → His spirit to be rotten, like Lucifer (from Luciel), and resembles Lucifer more than God.
13. What is the law?
14. The law: No sex with woman: Hawa until Adam's spirit reaches the seventh level with God's order.
15. Why? God gave the law to Adam to make him God's lover only; to make Adam's soul focused only on the Creator.
16. So to make the perfect first love (prototype love) between God and man.
17. Because Adam did not obey the law (did not keep the promise), Adam's spirit = rotten and flesh's DNA = rotten.

18. Spirit growth be stopped and rotten DNA inherited.
19. Cain's descendants' DNA closer to Satan's DNA because Cain's descendants did not give up Satan's DNA.
20. But Seth's descendant gave up Satan's DNA. Especially Noah did that, and Moses gave up Satan's DNA.
21. To solve the problem of sin, second Adam came to make the seventh-level spirit.
22. After 2nd trial failed by Satan's children, 3rd Adam came to the earth for completing God's plan

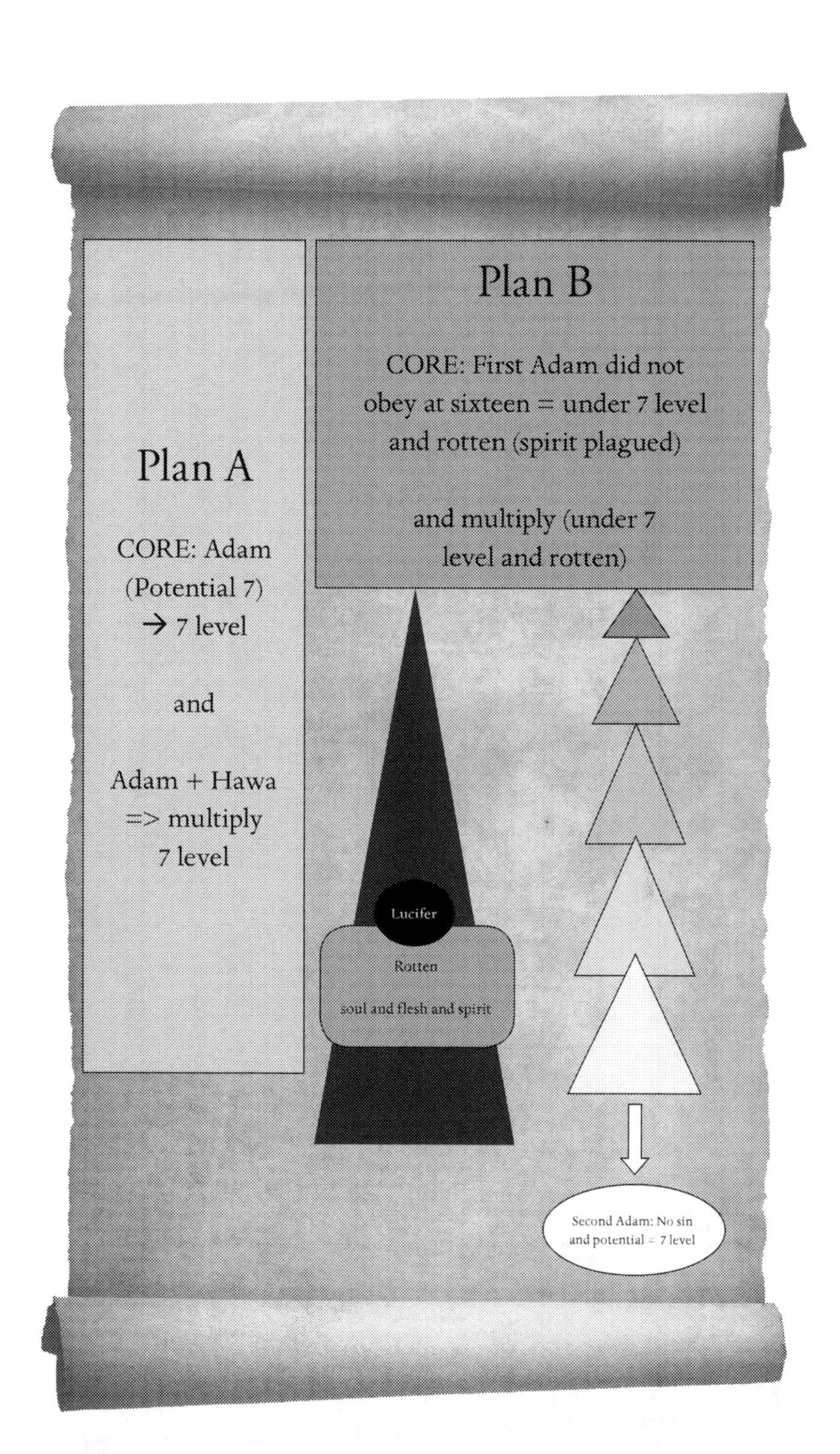
Plan A
CORE: Adam
(Potential 7)
→ 7 level
and
Adam + Hawa
=> multiply
7 level
Plan B
CORE: First Adam did not
obey at sixteen = under 7 level
and rotten (spirit plagued)
and multiply (under 7
level and rotten)
Lucifer
Rotten
soul and flesh and spirit
Second Adam: No sin
and potential = 7 level

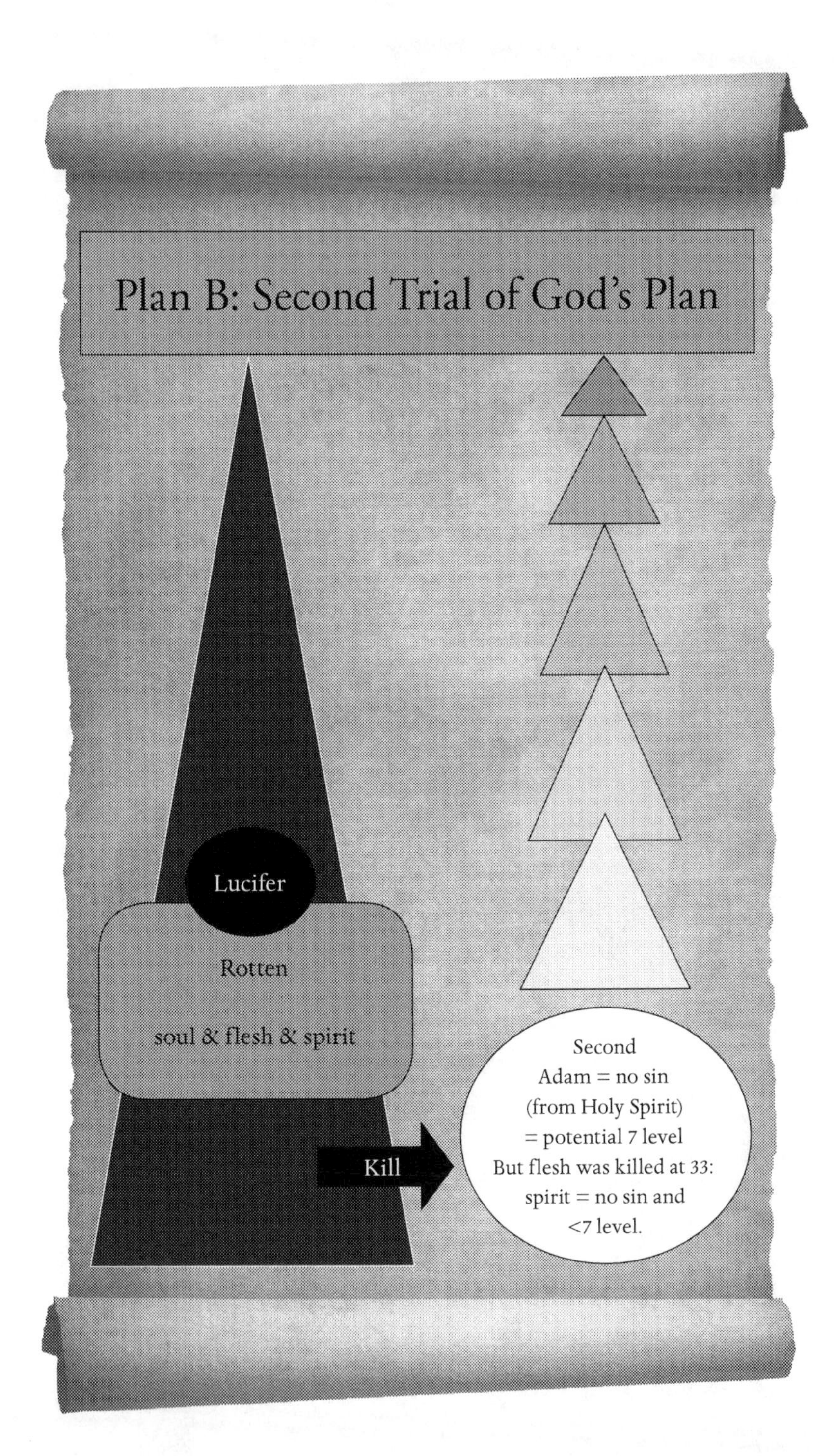
Plan B: Second Trial of God's Plan
Lucifer
Rotten
soul & flesh & spirit
Kill
Second
Adam = no sin
(from Holy Spirit)
= potential 7 level
But flesh was killed at 33:
spirit = no sin and
<7 level.

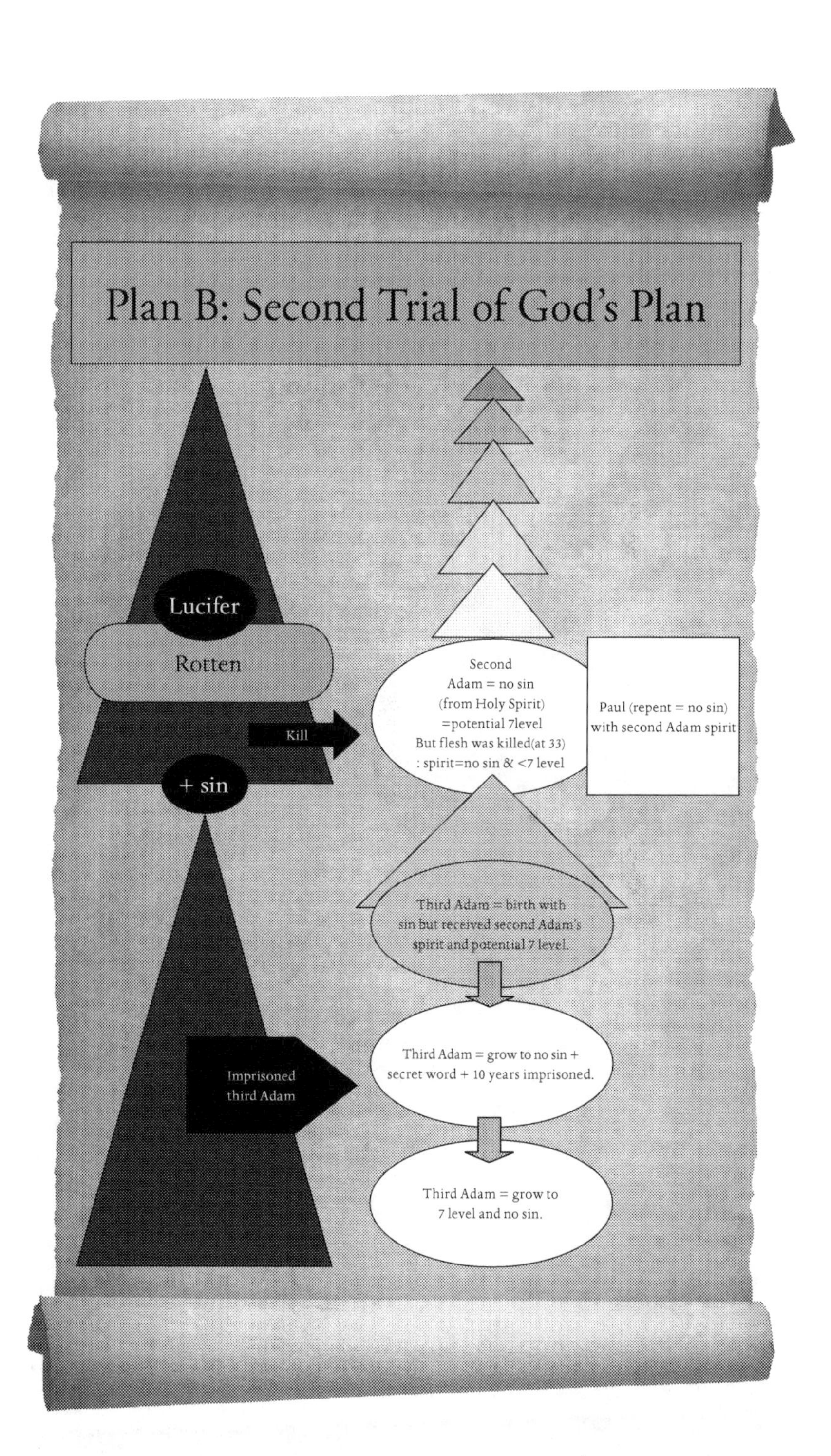
Plan B: Second Trial of God's Plan
Lucifer
Rotten
Kill
+ sin
Second
Adam = no sin
(from Holy Spirit)
=potential 7level
But flesh was killed(at 33)
: spirit=no sin & <7 level
Paul (repent = no sin)
with second Adam spirit
Third Adam = birth with
sin but received second Adam's
spirit and potential 7 level.
Imprisoned
third Adam
Third Adam = grow to no sin +
secret word + 10 years imprisoned.
Third Adam = grow to
7 level and no sin.

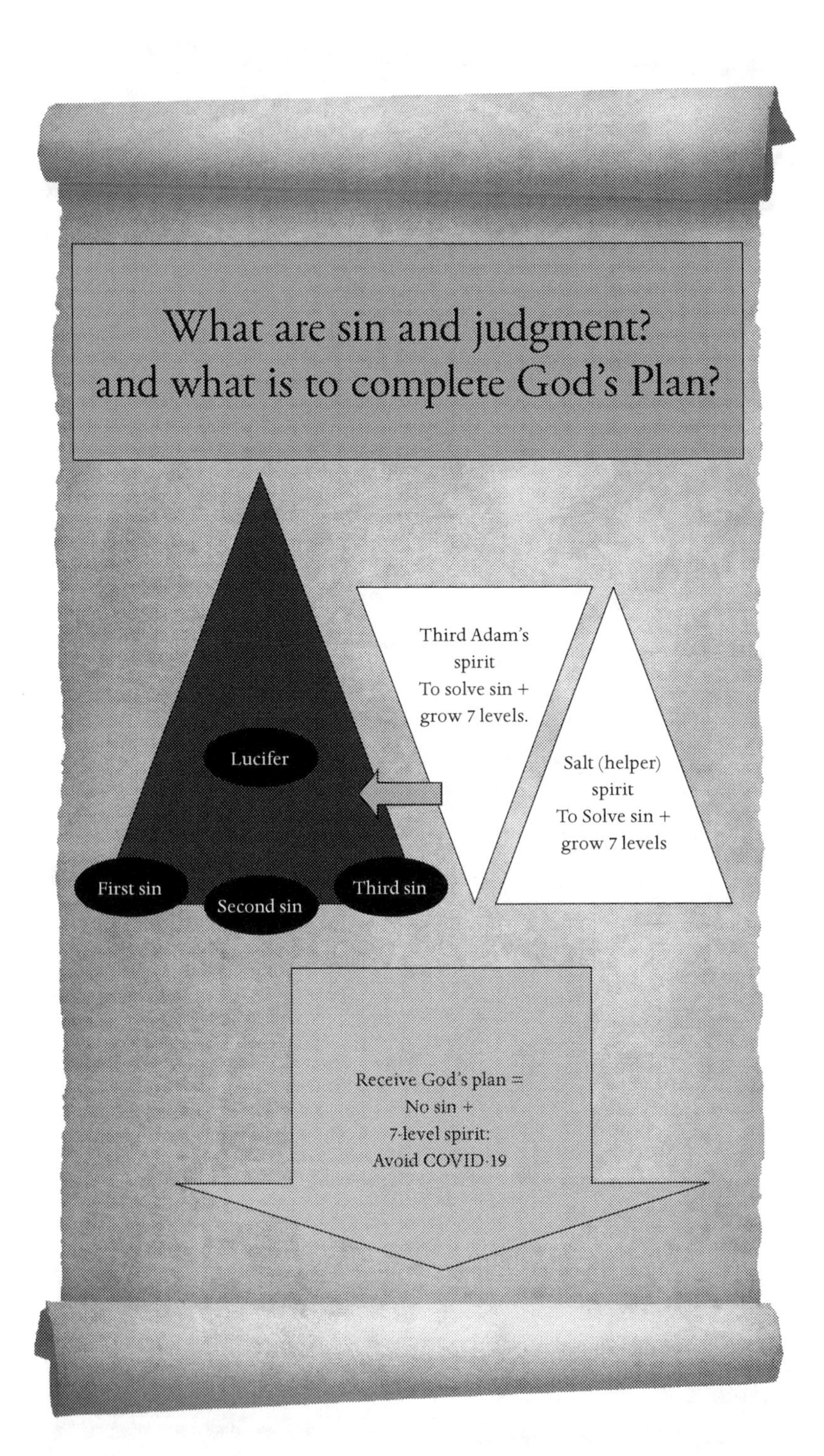
What are sin and judgment?
and what is to complete God's Plan?
Third Adam's
spirit
To solve sin +
grow 7 levels.
Lucifer
Salt (helper)
spirit
To Solve sin +
grow 7 levels
First sin
Second sin
Third sin
Receive God's plan =
No sin +
7-level spirit:
Avoid COVID-19

GOD'S MESSAGE

Satan's children are crowded.
Suffering's sound is heard by me.

The time of judgment is here. I will
destroy Satan and Satan's children and
their buildings, cities, and so on.
And I will rebuild the world
with God's plan.

VACCINE

#3

God's DNA

(DNA must receive God)

vs.

Satan's DNA

(DNA likely to receive Satan)

INTRODUCTION

From 1 Thessalonians 5:23:

And the very God of peace sanctify you wholly; and I pray God your whole spirit and soul and body be preserved blameless unto the coming of our Lord Jesus Christ.

Soul is a bridge of flesh and spirit. And soul has a mind, heart, and thinking. The heart receives signs from the flesh or spirit. Thinking has a choice of signs. If more God's DNA, thinking chooses more of God's signs.

If more Satan's DNA, thinking chooses more of Satan's signs.

#1 GOD'S PLAN

First Adam was not be fruitful because of Satan's interference.

So first son of Adam and Hawa, Cain, has more of Satan's DNA

(Satan DNA>God DNA in himself) than their second son, Abel.

So Cain killed Abel because of receiving Satan's sign.

In response,

God's plan started from third Seth.

From Seth to Noah, Abraham, Isaac, Jacob, David, Solomon to

Second Adam, Jesus: Satan's DNA decreases, and God's DNA increases,

So second Adam's Satan DNA = zero,

and the Holy Spirit gave birth to second Adam.

But second Adam was killed at thirty-three by Satan. God's plan B was blocked. So to complete God's plan, God sent third Adam to earth. Third Adam completed God's plan while humankind slept.

God's last plan was for the third Adam to multiply and defeat Satan and Satan's kingdom by judgment. COVID-19 is the most powerful of the judgments.

God said to us, "COVID19 is judgement of the sin. where sins are, judgement must be there. Receive God's plan. That is the only vaccine for COVID-19."*<I received this message from God when I was praying.>*

GOD'S PLAN → SATAN'S
DNA DECREASES
DNA
DNA

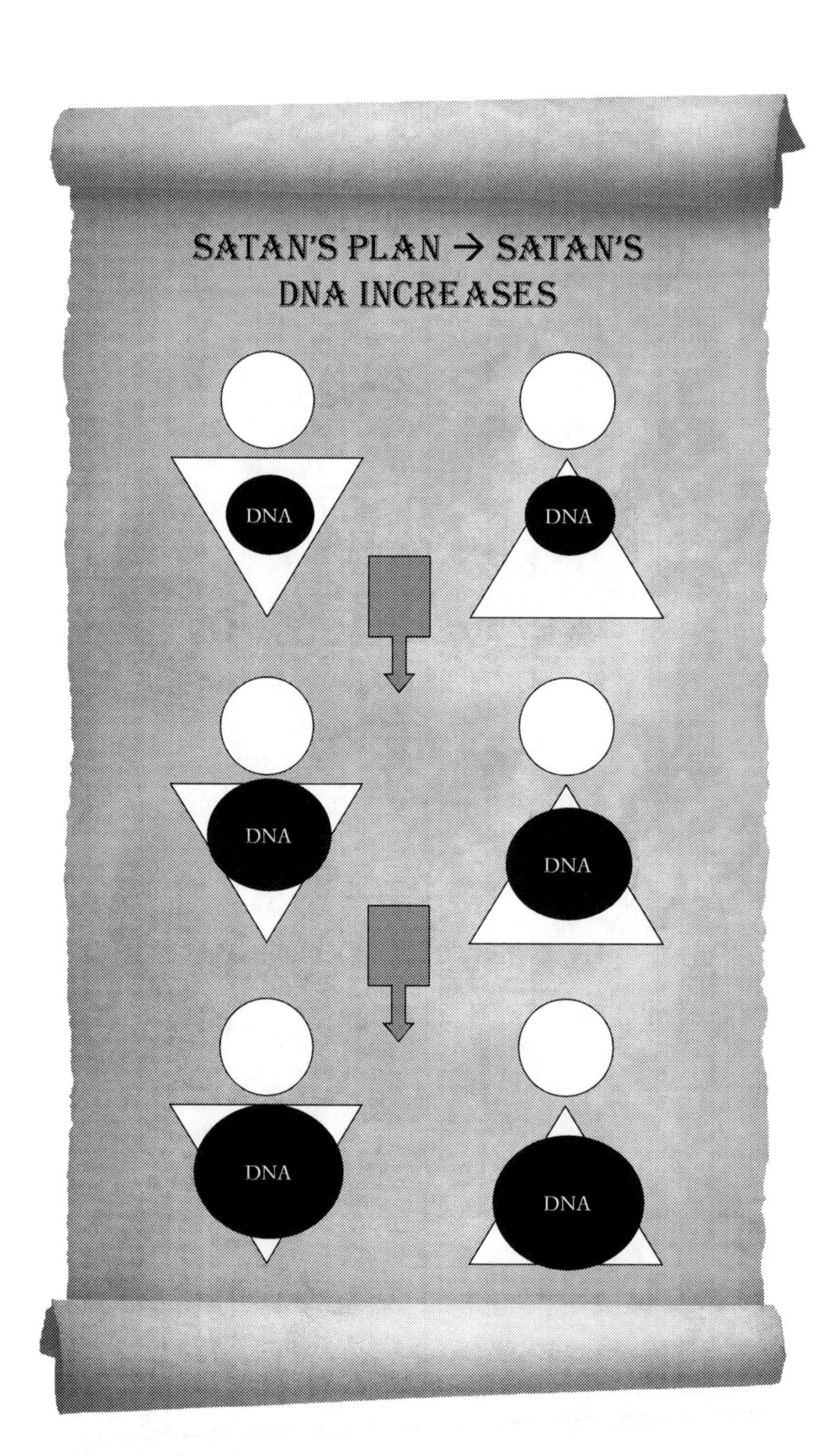
SATAN'S PLAN → SATAN'S DNA INCREASES
DNA
DNA
DNA
DNA
DNA
DNA

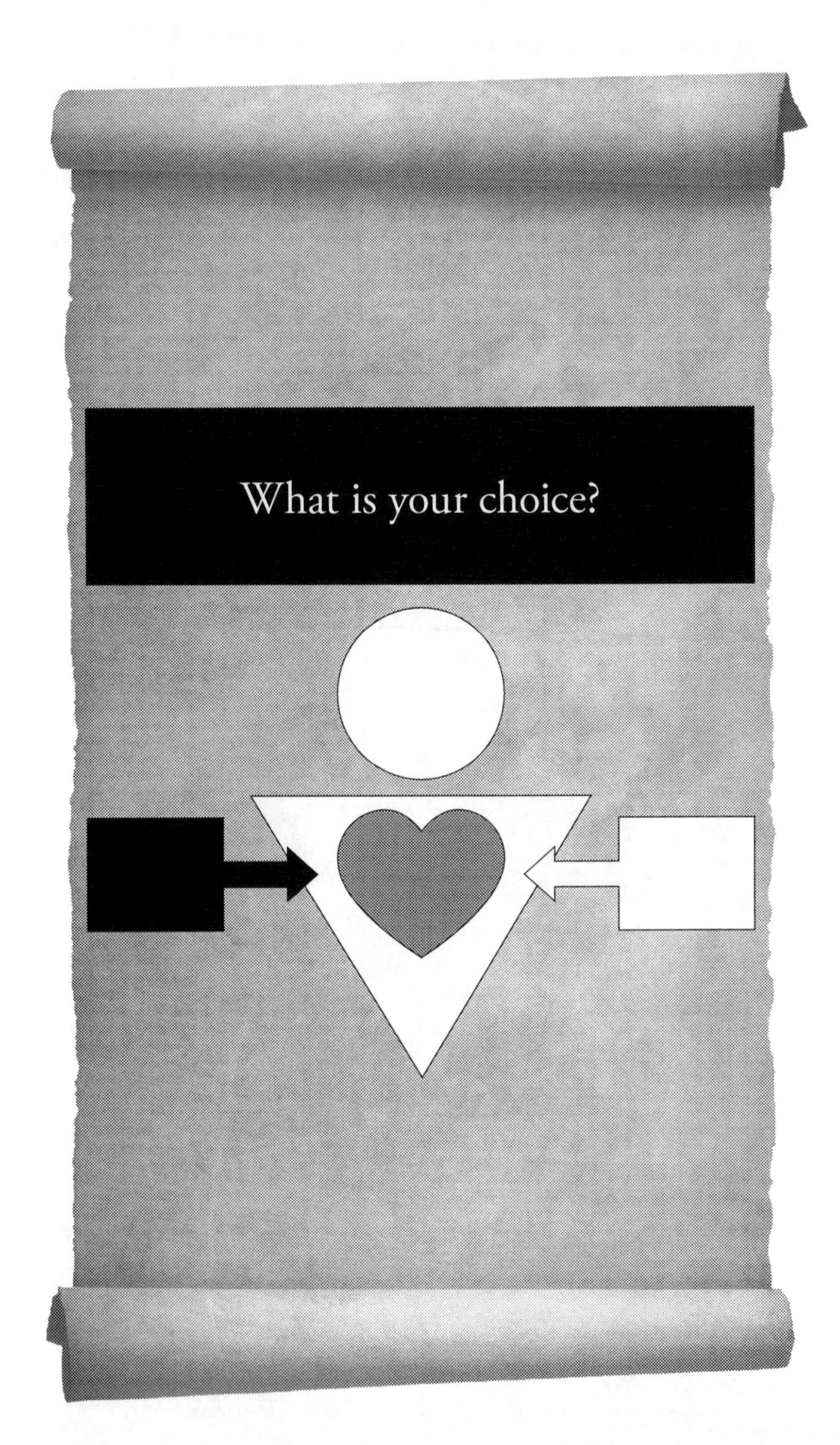
What is your choice?

VACCINE
#4
DRAMA IN
REVERSE:
GOD'S PLAN VS
SATAN'S PLAN

#1

Big Shock

From stone to stone, from man to man,
from science to science,
Are linked to Satan, Lucifer.

Where do you belong?
Accept anyone, all the world loves Satan,
Lucifer.
It's just we do not know that!

Do not know God's plan?
Satan: Lucifer is king of the world.
You love Satan.
You just do not know that.

Before being Lucifer, Luciel is loved mostly by God, Trinity.

But after listening to God's plan to create man's spirit,

Luciel was rotten.
That is singularity of all suffering and all sins.

Lucifer was against God's plan.
Finally, Lucifer make Adam and Hawa to be rotten.
From Adam and Hawa,
Especially from Cain, sin was exploded.
So for six thousand years,
Lucifer make himself the king of the world
And the father of the world.

No exceptions for a long time.

So Lucifer's children
Make the world to be only for man's flesh.

Only flesh's eye,
Only flesh's ear.

Only to eat,
Only to sleep,
Only to drink,
Only to have sex,
Do men live.

Men love only Lucifer.

Satan's children are against God's plan.
Made men commit sins.

Satan prevented men's flesh from being fruitful of Spirit.
Made men to live only for flesh's wants.
Only obsessed with what is visible.

Men blocked the signal of the Spirit
And amplified only the signal of body.
So that broke the relation with God.

#2

Where Did It Go Wrong?

Fear, envy, and jealousy of a better being made archangel Luciel to be rotten. So Luciel became Lucifer. Lucifer made first Adam and Hawa to be rotten. This is the singular point of sins.

#3

What Did God Do?

God is dead?
God waited for the time to reverse this.
God made God's laws.
Example: Before the time, do not judge.
God waited for the time of judgment.
First of all, God made second Adam to solve first Adam's sins.
And he made third Adam to be fruitful to God's plan.
And it succeeded from 1978 to 2018.
Now at 2020.6.1–2023.6.1,
Last judgment will be.

#4

Last Judgment

Now is like Moses' time.
God promised to give Abraham the Promised Land.

God listened to the sound of Israel's suffering in Egypt.
So God sent Moses to Israel,
And made Moses to say,
"Let my Israel to leave Egypt."
But Egypt's Pharaoh said no.
In response,
God caused nine disasters.

Still Pharaoh said no.
God was ready to cause a last disaster.
Like this.
Now, 2020, the world seems to be the world of Satan and his children.
Satan—Lucifer—is the king of the world.
For this, Lucifer gave all power to his children.
Example: The richest people in the world are children of Satan.

After God sent the first Adam, four thousand years went by, and then the second Adam came.
And after the second Adam, two thousand years passed.
A total of six thousand years went by.
There are a thousand years left for God's plan completion

(like 1 week = Mon + Tue + Wed + Thur + Fri + Sat + Sun)
From out of Eden to return to Eden,
six thousand years are needed.

For return to Eden,
God was ready to issue the last judgment to destroy Satan, Satan's children, and Satan's kingdom.

Last judgment's time is between 2020 and 2023.
Disaster: especially COVID-19 + alpha

Like Moses's time,
Before God caused the last disaster, God gave the way to avoid disaster to only Israel:
Putting lamb's blood on the doorpost.

After that, God, at midnight, struck down all the firstborn in Egypt, including the firstborn son of Pharaoh.

And Pharaoh surrendered to God.

#5

Prediction

God's last judgment will rise between 2020 and 2023.

Only those who receive the third Adam and God's plan will avoid the last judgment.

But if they do not receive that, never will they avoid last judgment.

Satan's children will make a vaccine for COVID-19. But it will not work.

This story is from Trinity.

GOD'S PLAN #3

PATTERN
OF
HISTORY

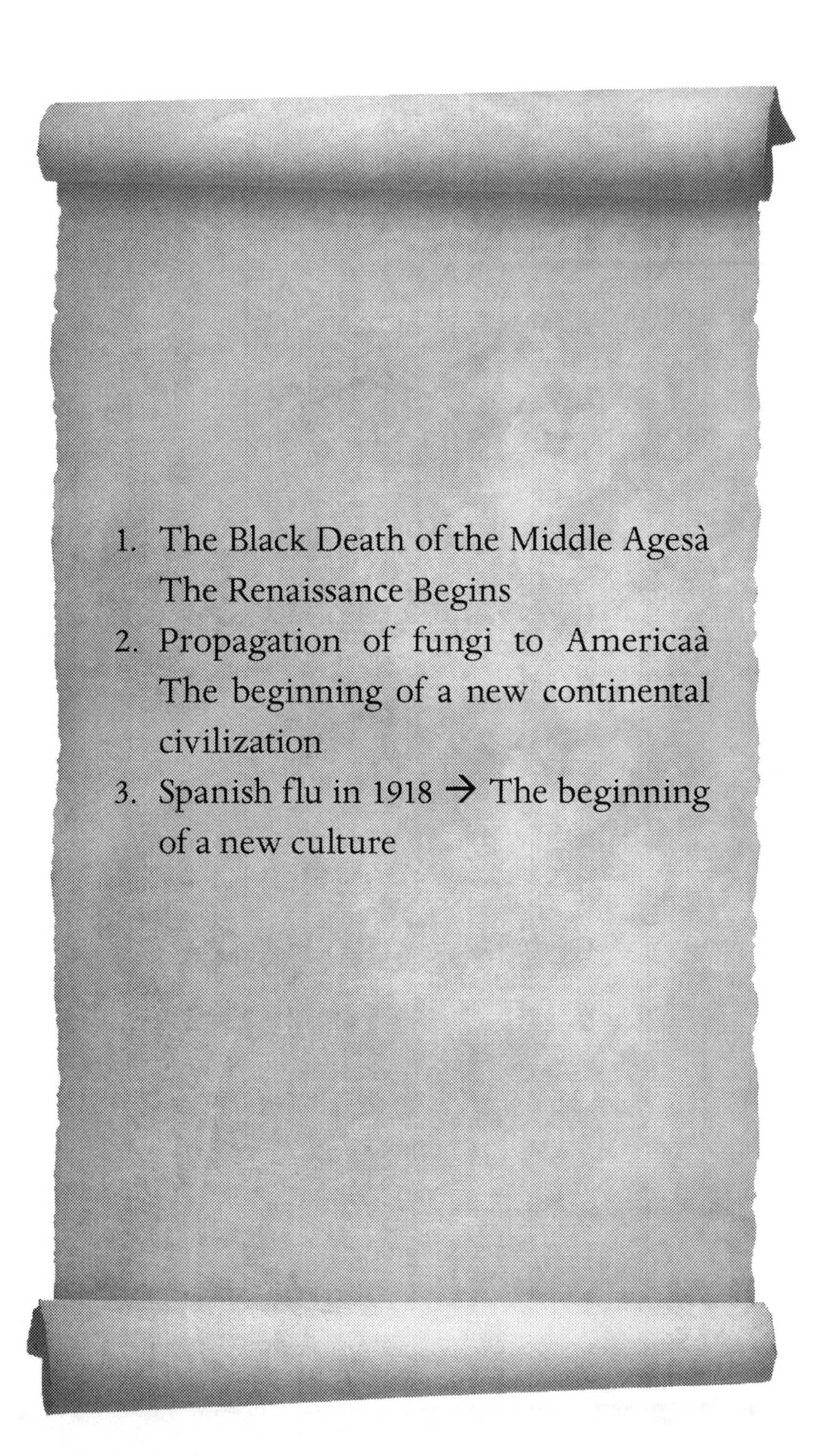

1. The Black Death of the Middle Agesà The Renaissance Begins
2. Propagation of fungi to Americaà The beginning of a new continental civilization
3. Spanish flu in 1918 → The beginning of a new culture

Spanish Flu	COVID-19
Primary fashion: Spring 1918	First phase: December 2019 to May 2020
Second pandemic: August 1918 to spring 1919; deaths: 50 million	Second phase: From June 1 to July 31, 2020: warm up. From August 1, 2020 to June 1,2023: full-scale epidemic spread

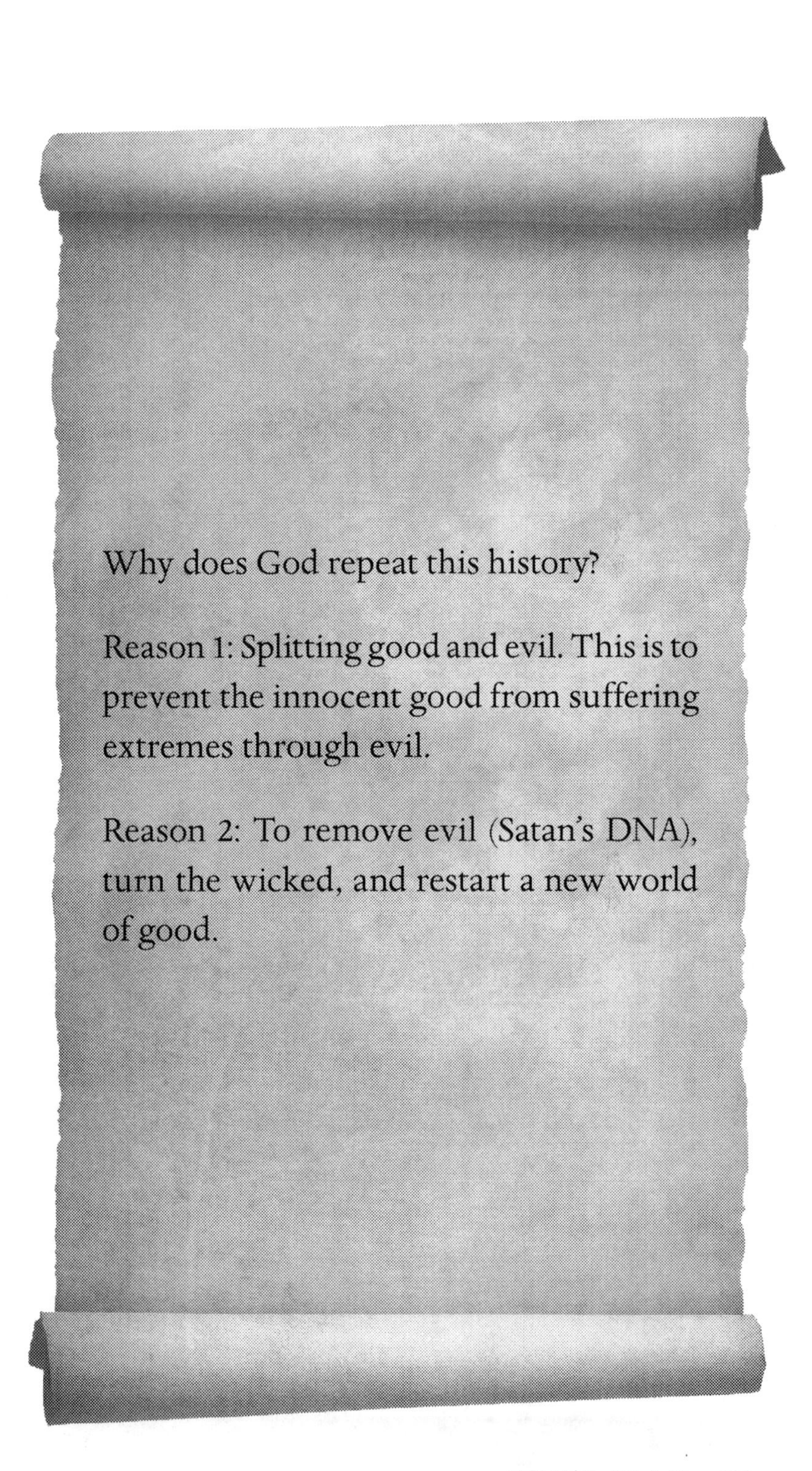

Why does God repeat this history?

Reason 1: Splitting good and evil. This is to prevent the innocent good from suffering extremes through evil.

Reason 2: To remove evil (Satan's DNA), turn the wicked, and restart a new world of good.

EPILOGUE

I was born in Korea. In Korea there is mandatory military duty. I fulfilled my military duties in prison. Korea is afraid of prisons, and people who work in prisons are reluctant to let people know where they work. I announced the following at a military conference: "Everyone can sin. Anyone can start again. In that sense, prisons are an important place, and those who work in prisons are good people. So everyone loves himself and loves his work." Come to know now it was God's plan.

While I was praying, I received this message from God.

On July 7, 2020, God said,

Everyone around the world has a COVID19 without exception. However, it is asymptomatic. If you do not accept God's plan, you will have the symptoms of COVID19 without exception.